OTTO GRAHAM, JIM BROWN,
MOTLEY, PAUL WARFIELD, DANTE LAVELLI,
OZZIE NEWSOME, MIKE MCCORMACK,
JIM RAY SMITH, JOE DELAMIELLEURE,
GENE HICKERSON, FRANK GATSKI,
LEN FORD, PAUL WIGGIN, BILL WILLIS,
JERRY SHERK, CLAY MATTHEWS, CHIP
BANKS, JIM HOUSTON, HANFORD DIXON,
FRANK MINNIFIELD,
WARREN LAHR, THOM

THE STORY OF THE CLEVELAND BROWNS

DARDEN, LOU GROZA, DON COCKROFT,
OTTO GRAHAM, JIM BROWN, MARION
MOTLEY, PAUL WARFIELD, DANTE LAVELLI,
OZZIE NEWSOME, MIKE MCCORMACK,
JIM RAY SMITH, JOE DELAMIELLEURE

THE STORY OF THE
CLEVELAND
BROWNS

BY JIM WHITING
CREATIVE EDUCATION / CREATIVE PAPERBACKS

PUBLISHED BY CREATIVE EDUCATION AND CREATIVE PAPERBACKS
P.O. BOX 227, MANKATO, MINNESOTA 56002
CREATIVE EDUCATION AND CREATIVE PAPERBACKS ARE IMPRINTS OF THE
CREATIVE COMPANY
WWW.THECREATIVECOMPANY.US

DESIGN AND PRODUCTION BY BLUE DESIGN (WWW.BLUEDES.COM)
ART DIRECTION BY RITA MARSHALL
PRINTED IN CHINA

PHOTOGRAPHS BY AP IMAGES (ASSOCIATED PRESS), GETTY IMAGES (SCOTT
BOEHM, NICK CAMMETT/DIAMOND IMAGES, JONATHAN DANIEL, DAVID
DERMER/DIAMOND IMAGES, STEPHEN DUNN, FOCUS ON SPORT, GEORGE
GOJKOVICH, BOB GOMEL/TIME & LIFE PICTURES, FRANK JANSKY/ICON
SPORTSWIRE, JIM MCISAAC, RONALD C. MODRA/SPORTS IMAGERY, NFL, HY
HY PESKIN/SI, PRO FOOTBALL HALL OF FAME/NFL, JOE ROBBINS, GEORGE
ROSE, PAUL SPINELLI, VIC STEIN, MATT SULLIVAN, TONY TOMSIC/NFL)

NAMES: WHITING, JIM, AUTHOR.
TITLE: THE STORY OF THE CLEVELAND BROWNS / JIM WHITING.
SERIES: NFL TODAY.
INCLUDES INDEX.
SUMMARY: THIS HIGH-INTEREST HISTORY OF THE NATIONAL FOOTBALL
LEAGUE'S CLEVELAND BROWNS HIGHLIGHTS MEMORABLE GAMES, SUMMARIZES
SEASONAL TRIUMPHS AND DEFEATS, AND FEATURES STANDOUT PLAYERS SUCH
AS JOE THOMAS.
IDENTIFIERS: LCCN 2018035583 / ISBN 978-1-64026-137-2 (HARDCOVER) / ISBN
978-1-62832-700-7 (PBK) / ISBN 978-1-64000-255-5 (EBOOK)
SUBJECTS: LCSH: CLEVELAND BROWNS (FOOTBALL TEAM: 1946-1995)—HISTORY—
JUVENILE LITERATURE. / CLEVELAND BROWNS (FOOTBALL TEAM: 1999-)—
HISTORY—JUVENILE LITERATURE. / FOOTBALL—UNITED STATES—HISTORY—
JUVENILE LITERATURE.
CLASSIFICATION: LCC GV956.C6 W47 2019 / DDC 796.332/640977132—DC23

FIRST EDITION HC 9 8 7 6 5 4 3 2 1
FIRST EDITION PBK 9 8 7 6 5 4 3 2 1

TABLE OF CONTENTS

GRIDIRON GREATS

GREATEST GAME
EVER

Just over three minutes remained in the 1950 National Football League (NFL) Championship Game. The Cleveland Browns trailed the Los Angeles Rams, 28–27. The Browns had the ball. But their star quarterback Otto Graham was tackled. He fumbled the ball. The Rams recovered it. "I wanted to dig a hole right in the middle of that stadium, crawl into it, and bury myself forever," Graham said after the game. "I figured that fumble cost us the game." On the sideline, coach Paul Brown reassured him. "Don't worry, we'll get it back," Brown said. "We're going to win." Cleveland's defense stopped the Rams in their tracks. The Browns

CLEVELAND BROWNS

9

LEFT: OTTO GRAHAM AND PAUL BROWN

took over. Less than two minutes were left. Graham ran for 14 yards. Then he completed three passes to put the ball on the Rams' 11-yard line. Cleveland kicker Lou Groza lined up for the short field goal. Would he make it? There was a reason the Browns were just one point behind the Rams. Earlier, there had been a bad snap on a try for the extra point after a touchdown. Groza had missed. In the sub-freezing temperatures, it could happen again.

Fortunately, the ball sailed through the uprights. The Browns now led, 30–28. Hundreds of happy fans swarmed from the stands. But the game wasn't over. Less than 20 seconds remained. The field was cleared. Cleveland kicked off. The Rams drove all the way to the 47-yard line. Los Angeles quarterback Norm Van Brocklin hurled the ball toward the end zone. Cleveland defensive back Warren Lahr jumped up. He grabbed the ball. But on the way down, intended receiver Glenn Davis tried to pull it away. The two men tumbled into the end zone. A hush fell over Municipal Stadium. The officials huddled to discuss the play. Graham recalled, "[The waiting] was terrible. We

GRIDIRON GREATS ⌄
GRAHAM IS GRAND

Otto Graham played basketball at Northwestern University. He even played for the National Basketball League's Rochester Royals. They won the 1946 championship. But football was his destiny. Northwestern football coach Pappy Waldorf discovered Graham. He watched Graham during an intramural football game. Graham became an outstanding passer. He sparked the Browns to the greatest 10-year period in NFL history. "I remember his tremendous peripheral vision and his great athletic skill, as well as his ability to throw a football far and accurately with just a flick of his arm," said coach Paul Brown. "Otto Graham was the greatest player in the game's history."

CLEVELAND BROWNS

11

LOU GROZA'S FIELD GOAL ATTEMPT

"I WANTED TO DIG A HOLE RIGHT IN THE MIDDLE OF THAT STADIUM, CRAWL INTO IT, AND BURY MYSELF FOREVER."

—OTTO GRAHAM ON CHAMPIONSHIP FUMBLE

didn't know what the referee was going to call.... What if they gave Davis the ball and a touchdown? And what if they called it a safety or something? That would have been two points and a tie game." The referee finally spoke. It was an interception. Game over. NFL commissioner Bert Bell called it "the greatest football game I've ever seen.... It was unfortunate that one of those two truly great teams had to lose."

In a way, the game was Cleveland past vs. Cleveland present. In 1937, the Rams had started operations in Cleveland. But they left for Los Angeles in 1946. Now, Cleveland belonged to the Browns.

LOU GROZA
OFFENSIVE TACKLE, KICKER

BROWNS SEASONS: 1946–59 (AS TACKLE), 1961–67 (AS KICKER)
HEIGHT: 6-FOOT-3
WEIGHT: 240 POUNDS

GRIDIRON GREATS ∨

THE TOE

Lou Groza was pro football's first great kicker. He was nicknamed "The Toe." Groza set many records for field goals attempted and made. He retired as the league's all-time leading scorer. Kicking is only half of The Toe's story. He was also one of the best left tackles in NFL history. His blocks protected Browns quarterbacks. He opened gaping holes for running backs. He was named to the Pro Bowl nine times during the 1950s. Today, the Browns' training facility sits at 76 Lou Groza Boulevard. The annual Lou Groza Award honors the best kicker in college football.

268

268 GAMES PLAYED

264 FIELD GOALS MADE

264

TOTAL DOMINATION

n 1944, a group of wealthy businessmen formed a new professional football league. It was called the All-American Football Conference (AAFC). The eight-team league began play in 1946. Arthur "Mickey" McBride purchased the Cleveland franchise. He hired Paul Brown as the team's coach. Brown had led Ohio State University to the 1942 national championship. He was very popular in the region. McBride held a name-the-team contest. Browns had the most votes. But Paul Brown said no. Panthers was the second choice. That name didn't work, though. An earlier Cleveland team had used that name before folding in 1933. The owner still held the rights to the name. He tried to sell those rights to McBride. McBride refused. Besides, Brown said, "That old Panthers team failed. I want no part of that

126

126 CAREER TOUCHDOWNS

118

118 GAMES PLAYED

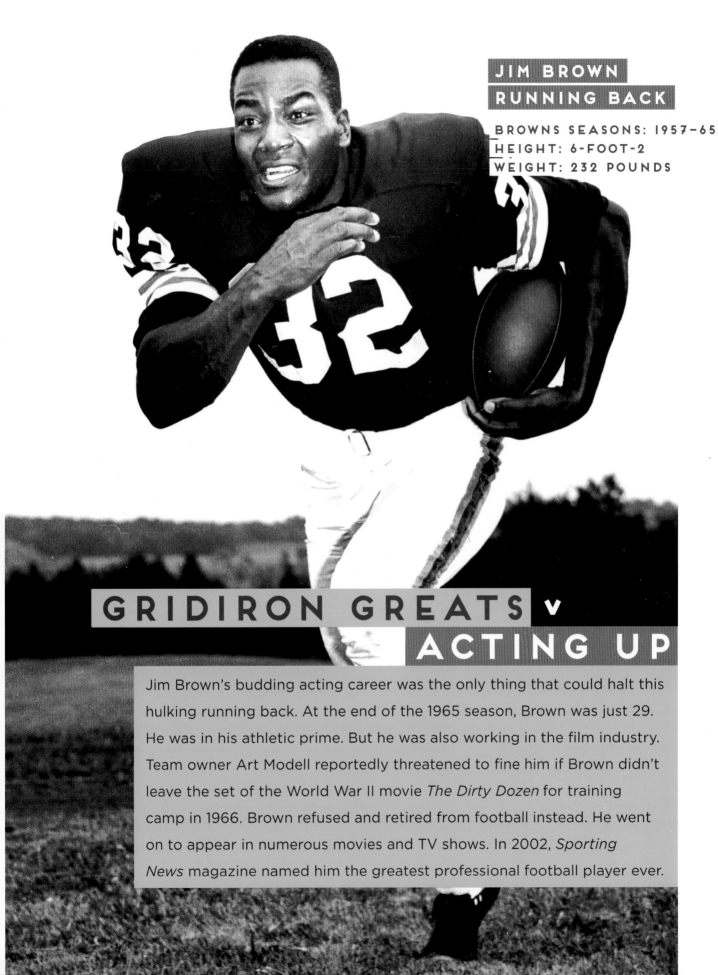

GRIDIRON GREATS v
ACTING UP

Jim Brown's budding acting career was the only thing that could halt this hulking running back. At the end of the 1965 season, Brown was just 29. He was in his athletic prime. But he was also working in the film industry. Team owner Art Modell reportedly threatened to fine him if Brown didn't leave the set of the World War II movie *The Dirty Dozen* for training camp in 1966. Brown refused and retired from football instead. He went on to appear in numerous movies and TV shows. In 2002, *Sporting News* magazine named him the greatest professional football player ever.

CLEVELAND BROWNS

name." McBride went back to the first choice: Browns.

Brown was clear about his goal for the team. "I want [the Browns] to be what the New York Yankees are in baseball, or what Ben Hogan is in golf," he said. In other words, the biggest name in the sport. To achieve this goal, Brown handpicked his roster. It featured several of his former college players. He also chose players he had both feared and admired as opponents. The most notable was Graham. Brown combined outstanding players with many coaching innovations. "Football would not be what it is without him," Cincinnati Bengals quarterback Ken Anderson said years later.

From the beginning, the Browns set the gold standard for the AAFC. In the league's four years, the Browns had a regular-season record of 47–4–3. They won the AAFC title every year. Graham threw pass after pass to lanky tight end Mac Speedie. Hulking fullback Marion Motley pounded the ball on the ground. The league folded after the 1949 season. The Browns and two other teams joined the NFL in 1950. Few believed that Cleveland's success could continue in its new league. Brown wasn't worried, though. His confidence inspired his players. They easily defeated the reigning NFL champion Philadelphia Eagles in the first game of the season. Graham threw for 346 yards and 3 touchdowns. He rushed for a fourth score.

"WE WERE SO FIRED UP. WE WOULD HAVE PLAYED THEM FOR A KEG OF BEER OR A CHOCOLATE MILKSHAKE."

—OTTO GRAHAM ON THE BROWNS' FIRST NFL GAME

"We were so fired up," he remembered. "We would have played them for a keg of beer or a chocolate milkshake."

The Browns compiled a 10–2 season. It culminated in the last-moment championship over the Rams. After that, Cleveland won the NFL Eastern Conference title for the next five years. It captured two more NFL championships. The 1955 NFL Championship Game against the Rams was Graham's last. He threw two touchdowns. He ran for two more. Then he left the game to a standing ovation from the rival fans. He had led his team to one of the most dominating decades in any professional sport. During that time, the Browns won 114 games while losing just 20.

A NEW SUPERSTAR

JIM BROWN

After Graham left, Cleveland experienced its first losing season. Soon, a new superstar emerged. In 1957, the Browns drafted fullback Jim Brown. He was a 6-foot-2 and 232-pound powerhouse. With a mix of speed and strength, he ran for 942 yards and scored 10 touchdowns as a rookie. The following year, he nearly doubled those numbers. By the end of his NFL career, Brown had rushed for 12,312 yards and 106 touchdowns. He won eight league rushing titles. He also hauled in 20 touchdown passes.

Brown's heroics took some of the pressure off the string of quarterbacks

GRIDIRON GREATS v

HOMETOWN BOY MAKES GOOD

Bernie Kosar grew up in nearby Youngstown. He dreamed of playing for the Browns. The feeling was mutual. Kosar didn't throw like most quarterbacks. He launched the ball with an awkward, half-sidearm motion. Still, he usually found his mark. During the 1990 and 1991 seasons, he set an NFL record. He completed 308 consecutive passes without throwing an interception. His abilities on the field and his friendliness off it endeared Kosar to fans. Municipal Stadium often rocked to the sound of fans singing their own version of the pop hit "Louie, Louie." They changed the catchy refrain to "Bernie, Bernie."

129

129 CAREER TOUCHDOWNS

126

126 GAMES PLAYED

who tried to replace Graham. The team rode Jim Brown's shoulders to the East Division title in 1957. Brown couldn't win the league championship alone. The team lost to the Detroit Lions. It returned to the playoffs in 1958. But the late 1950s and early '60s were ultimately disappointing. Fans were not accustomed to losing. Art Modell bought the team in 1961. He blamed Coach Brown for the decline. Brown's no-nonsense style rubbed some the wrong way. When the team finished 1962 at 7–6–1, Modell fired Brown. Blanton Collier was the new coach. Collier's looser style led to back-to-back 10-win seasons in 1963 and 1964. Brown rushed for 1,863 yards in 1963. That set an NFL single-season record. The Browns met the Baltimore Colts in the 1964 NFL Championship Game. They stifled the Colts' star quarterback, Johnny Unitas. Cleveland won, 27–0.

In 1965, Brown rushed for more than 1,500 yards. For the fourth time in his career, he was named the NFL's Most Valuable Player (MVP). He led the team back to the NFL Championship Game. There, the Browns lost to the

JIM BROWN

Green Bay Packers. Afterward, the 30-year-old running back retired. Brown left as the NFL's all-time leading rusher. Nearly two decades would pass before anyone topped Brown's total yardage. "It is possible that had he continued to play, he would have put all the league's rushing records so far out of reach that they would have been only a distant dream ... to the runners who followed him," *Sports Illustrated* reporter Peter King later noted.

1969 GAME AGAINST THE PACKERS

GRIDIRON GREATS
A SHINING LIGHT

Joe Thomas was a bright spot in Cleveland. He finished second to Adrian Peterson in voting for 2007 Rookie of the Year. He was selected for the Pro Bowl in each of his first 10 years. Only four other players have accomplished that. All are in the Hall of Fame. Joe was known for his consistency. "Joe is a warrior," said coach Hue Jackson in 2016. "This team is still together because of him and what he brings to that locker room each and every week after games and before games." During the 2017 season, he became the first player to reach 10,000 consecutive snaps since joining the league.

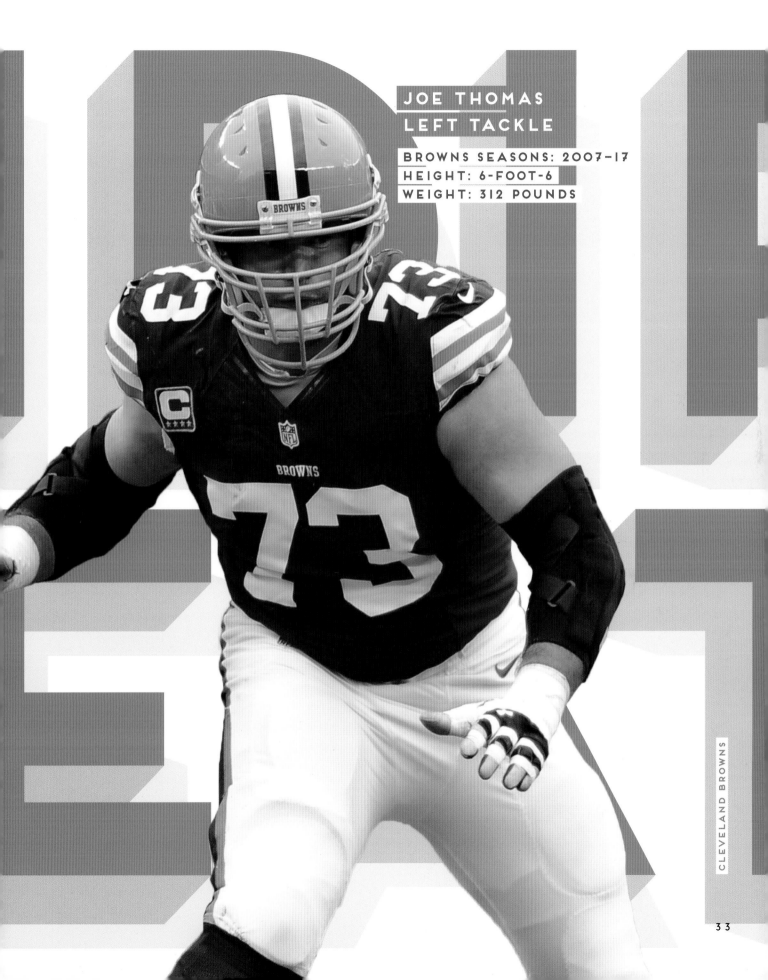

JOE THOMAS
LEFT TACKLE

BROWNS SEASONS: 2007-17
HEIGHT: 6-FOOT-6
WEIGHT: 312 POUNDS

CLEVELAND BROWNS

Running back Leroy Kelly
tried to fill Brown's shoes. Kelly's fast feet and receiver
Paul Warfield's sure hands propelled the Browns to the
NFL Championship Game in 1968 and 1969. They lost
both times. Cleveland made the playoffs in 1971 and
1972. The team struggled through most of the rest of the
1970s. Then the Browns rebounded. They played in the
postseason in 1980 and 1982. Both times, they lost in
the first round.

BERNIE KOSAR

"THE DRIVE" AND "THE FUMBLE"

The situation improved in 1985. The team drafted a hometown hero. He was quarterback Bernie Kosar. In 1986, Kosar led the Browns to a 12–4 record. One of his favorite targets was tight end Ozzie Newsome. The team faced the New York Jets in the playoffs. Fans groaned when the Jets took a 20–10 lead. Yet another playoff loss seemed likely. But Cleveland scored a touchdown and a field goal. The game went into overtime. Mark Moseley's 27-yard field goal gave the Browns a 23–20 win. It was the team's first playoff victory in 17 years.

Only the Denver Broncos stood between Cleveland and Super Bowl XXI. Kosar threw a 48-yard touchdown pass in the fourth quarter. That put the

Browns up 20–13. Denver misplayed the kickoff. They had to start from their own two-yard line. But Broncos quarterback John Elway calmly led his team 98 yards down the field. They tied the score. This series of 15 plays became known as "The Drive." The game went to overtime. A short field goal gave Denver the win.

The following season, the conference championship again pitted Cleveland against Denver. Kosar led a late rally. The Browns overcame an 18-point deficit to tie the score. But Denver answered. The Broncos took a seven-point lead. The Browns marched down the field. With one minute left, reliable Browns running back Earnest Byner took a handoff. He was just eight yards from the goal line. A Broncos cornerback knocked the ball out of Byner's hands. The Broncos recovered the fumble. Again the Browns were defeated. "It's tough to come back and tie the game and then lose," Kosar said afterwards. The game became known as "The Fumble." The two teams met again for the conference title two years later. Denver led from start to finish.

The 1990s began with four losing seasons in a row. Kosar was released in 1993. His departure upset many Browns fans. Then rumors started that owner Art Modell was thinking of moving the team. In November 1995, those rumors were confirmed. Modell announced that the franchise was moving to Baltimore. There, the Browns would become the Ravens. Reaction was swift.

QUARTERBACK BRIAN SIPE

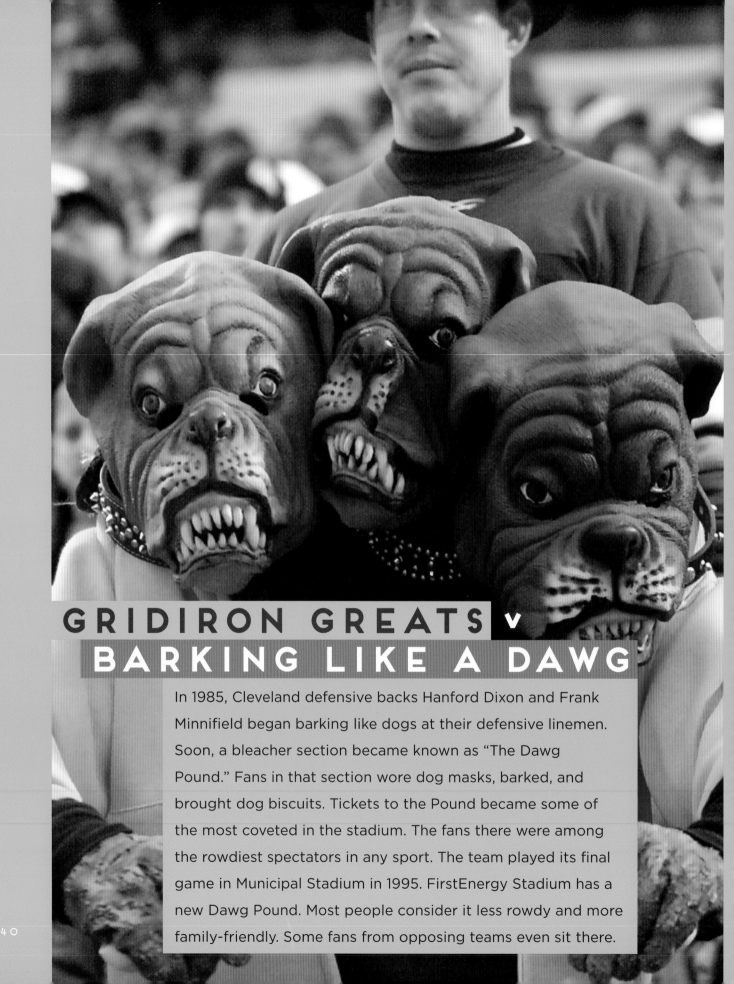

GRIDIRON GREATS v
BARKING LIKE A DAWG

In 1985, Cleveland defensive backs Hanford Dixon and Frank Minnifield began barking like dogs at their defensive linemen. Soon, a bleacher section became known as "The Dawg Pound." Fans in that section wore dog masks, barked, and brought dog biscuits. Tickets to the Pound became some of the most coveted in the stadium. The fans there were among the rowdiest spectators in any sport. The team played its final game in Municipal Stadium in 1995. FirstEnergy Stadium has a new Dawg Pound. Most people consider it less rowdy and more family-friendly. Some fans from opposing teams even sit there.

More than 100 lawsuits were filed, by both fans and the city of Cleveland. The NFL and city officials talked. Eventually, they came to an agreement. The league promised to bring a new Browns team to Cleveland by 1999. It would help fund a new stadium, too. Cleveland would keep the Browns' legacy. This included the team's name, colors, and history.

RUNNING BACK ERIC METCALF

THE BROWNS RETURN

T he "New Browns" began play in 1999. It was technically an expansion team with new players. Still, Cleveland embraced the team. More than 73,000 fans crammed into the new Cleveland Browns Stadium for the first game. But they were disappointed. The Browns were crushed 43–0 by the Pittsburgh Steelers. The offense managed only 40 total yards.

The Browns didn't record a victory until Week 8. At last, they triumphed over the Saints in New Orleans. Rookie quarterback Tim Couch's late-game heroics renewed the team's hopes for the future.

CLEVELAND BROWNS

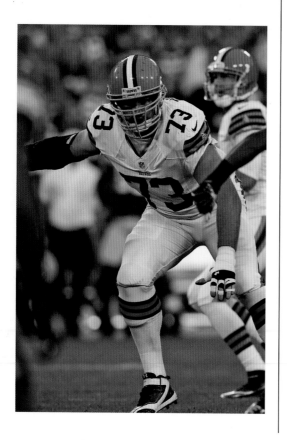

LEFT: JOE THOMAS

The Browns were behind by two points. Just two seconds remained. Couch launched a game-winning 56-yard Hail Mary pass to receiver Kevin Johnson. "It's a memory I'll never forget," Couch said. "I can remember [New Orleans coach] Mike Ditka lying on the carpet and seeing him as I was running down the sideline. That was probably the best part of all."

But Cleveland enjoyed victory only once more that season. Unfortunately, the 2–14 record set the tone for the next 18 years. The team had winning records just twice. It squeezed into the playoffs only once. In the 2002 Wild Card, Pittsburgh scored the game-winning touchdown with 58 seconds remaining. Five years later, Cleveland went 10–6. But it missed the playoffs. That season also marked the arrival of Joe Thomas. He would become one of the greatest offensive tackles of all time.

In 2014, the Browns won seven games. But they sank to 3–13 in 2015. They ended the next season with just one win. Fans thought things couldn't get worse. They were wrong. The Browns failed to win a single game in 2017. They became just the second NFL team to hold that dubious distinction in a 16-game season. As a joke, several thousand fans held a parade. They honored the team's "perfect season."

During this losing stretch, the Browns tried 27 different quarterbacks in addition to Couch. They burned through eight coaches. Still, the Browns looked forward to 2018.

RUNNING BACK TRENT RICHARDSON

WIDE RECEIVER ANTONIO CALLAWAY

They retained coach Hue Jackson for a third season. They had two of the top four picks in the draft. Plus, they had a whopping $100 million to spend on free agents. They rebounded to win seven games.

The Browns have fallen on tough times. But they have a proud heritage in the NFL. Few other teams can boast three players who accomplished as much as Otto Graham, Lou Groza, and Jim Brown. Fans celebrated with the Browns during the championship seasons of their glory days. They encouraged the team as it struggled in recent years, too. Those fans will cheer their Browns to the Super Bowl, no matter how long it takes them to get there.

AAFC CHAMPIONSHIPS

1946, 1947, 1948, 1949

NFL CHAMPIONSHIPS

1950, 1954, 1955, 1964

WEBSITES

CLEVELAND BROWNS

https://www.clevelandbrowns.com/

NFL: CLEVELAND BROWNS TEAM PAGE

http://www.nfl.com/teams/clevelandbrowns/profile?team=CLE

CLEVELAND BROWNS

INDEX

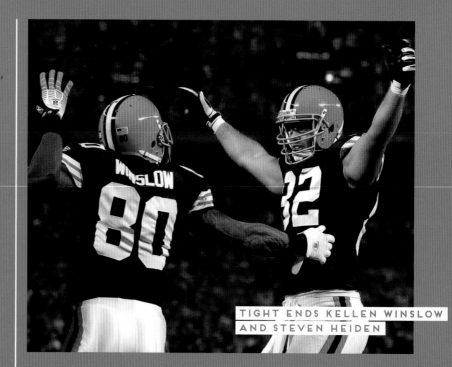

TIGHT ENDS KELLEN WINSLOW AND STEVEN HEIDEN